Discover & Learn

Stone Age to Celts

Years 3-4

This Teacher Book is the perfect companion to CGP's 'Stone Age to Celts' Activity Book for Years 3-4.

It contains a range of useful resources, including answers, information for teachers, prompts and guidance for pupils, and suggestions for extension activities.

It's ideal for helping your pupils explore the KS2 History topic 'Changes in Britain from the Stone Age to the Iron Age'.

History and Prehistory

Stone Age to Celts: Activity Book p.2-3

Primary sources present us with information. They don't lie. We can misinterpret them, e.g. by thinking that an axe is a knife, but the source itself doesn't give false information.

Pupil Guidance:

Ask pupils to think about what we use tools for today — cutting, breaking, scraping. This can help us to imagine how these objects might have been used then:

"Which one of these might you use to cut up your dinner? Which might you use to drive a peg into the ground?"

A and B are actually both flint arrowheads and C is a stone axe.

History and Prehistory

We find out about history using sources. A primary source is something from the period we study. A secondary source is a record about a primary source.

Have a look at these sources. They're tools or weapons from the Stone Age.

A B C

These are made from flint. This is made from stone.

Are these primary or secondary sources? Tick the correct answer.

primary ☑ secondary ☐

What tools or weapons do you think they are? Why do you think this?

I think A is a spearhead because it's got a sharp, pointy end.

I think B is an arrowhead because it's shaped to a sharp point and has a bit that you could attach wood to.

I think C is an axe because it's got a sharp edge but looks heavy.

Using these sources, what can you say about what tools and weapons in the Stone Age were made of?

The tools and weapons were made of flint and stone.

We can misinterpret a situation if we don't have the full picture. For example, we have evidence of early human habitation of the south of England, but none from Scotland and the north of England. However we cannot infer from this that humans definitely did not settle further north. Any evidence may have been destroyed by glaciation. Absence of evidence is not evidence of absence.

History and Prehistory: National Curriculum Aims

- Understand the methods of historical enquiry.
- Understand how evidence is used to make historical claims.
- Understand why there are different interpretations of the past.

Primary sources might not tell you the whole story.

The sources on page 2 give you information about what tools and weapons were used in the Stone Age.

Does this mean that these were the only tools and weapons used? Tick one box. Explain your answer.

Yes ☐ No ☑

I think this because *there might be tools or weapons that didn't survive or that haven't been discovered yet.*

Read page 2 of the Study Book.

Apart from tools and weapons, what else might historians have found that tells them about life in Britain in the Stone Age?

Hint: In the Stone Age, people couldn't write.

They might have found *bones / clothes / drawings on cave walls / carved pictures, etc.*

In this box, draw or write some things that historians in the future might discover from our time. What will it tell them about how we live?

What they might discover:	What it will tell them:
• *clothes*	• *what we wore*
• *toys*	• *what we played with*
• *bones*	• *what our bodies were like*
• *cars*	• *that we drove around*
• *buildings*	• *what our buildings were like*

"I know that archaeologists and historians use primary and secondary sources to find out about the past."

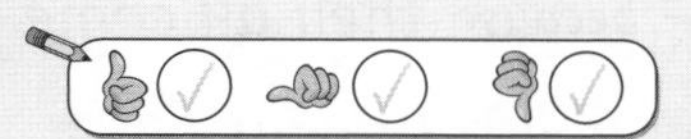

Extension Idea

Show pupils a clip from the daily news. Discuss whether it shows the way we would want to be remembered/judged. Is it truly representative of life in Britain today? Is it a primary or a secondary source?

Extension Idea (continued)

Now ask pupils to create a 'time capsule' — either real, drawn or written — that represents how they think their society should be remembered. Why have they included what they have? Does their record differ from the news clip? If so, how, and why?

How We Discover Prehistory

Stone Age to Celts: Activity Book p.4-5

Organic things — things that were once part of a living organism, such as wood, or hair — decay because they are in an environment where fungi and bacteria can break them down. However, organic objects survive longer if they are in an anaerobic (oxygen-less) environment, such as a peat bog.

4

How We Discover Prehistory

Most things that are made from plants and animals will rot away over time.

For example, wool and paper will rot away. (Paper comes from trees.)

Many things that are man-made will not rot away.

Things made of plastic and glass will not rot away.

Look around the room you are in. Think about all of the things in it. Now imagine the room being discovered in 10 000 years' time. The building would have fallen down a long time ago, and been buried under soil and earth.

What things in the room do you think would still be there for archaeologists to find? Explain why these things would survive.

I think that archaeologists would find my pen, my ruler, the trays, the chairs, the computer and my water bottle because they are made of man-made things like plastic and glass which don't rot away.

What things do you think wouldn't survive for archaeologists to find? Explain why not.

I think that my books, our paintings, my jumper, my scarf and the posters on the wall wouldn't survive because they all come from plants or animals, so they will rot away.

Pupil Guidance:

"Look around the room and see what each object is made of. Is it man-made or does it come from plants and animals? Does this mean that it will survive for 10 000 years or rot away?"

Extension Idea

Ask pupils to imagine what a future archaeologist would think about our lives if they only found the things that didn't rot. They might have no idea, for example, whether we wore clothes or didn't. What is there that wouldn't rot, that would tell them about how we lived? (E.g. computers — but how would they access the data on computers?)

Extension Idea

Ötzi the Ice Man was an incredible find because he was so well preserved — most animal tissue rots away. Pupils could use the Internet to research the discovery of Ötzi.

How We Discover Prehistory: National Curriculum Aims

- Understand the methods of historical enquiry.
- Understand how evidence is used to make historical claims.
- Understand why there are different interpretations of the past.

Some primary sources can be misleading...

The year is 12 050. An ancient classroom from 2014 has been discovered. Unexpectedly, a page of an exercise book has survived. Read what it says...

> ...Suddenly a huge asteroid struck the bridge of the spaceship. There was a loud crack, and all the lights flickered on and off. 'All officers to the stardrive section!' yelled the Captain, 'and turn on the force field!'

Tick 'Yes' or 'No' below to show which sentences you agree with.

The source proves that people in 2014 had spaceships.	Yes ☐	No ☑
The source proves that people in 2014 wrote stories.	Yes ☐	No ☑
The source proves nothing without other sources.	Yes ☑	No ☐

Read page 5 of the Study Book. Explain how archaeologists can tell how old something is by how deep it is buried.

The deeper something is buried in the ground, the older it is.

An archaeologist found a stone tool buried in the ground next to a bone.

How could the archaeologist find out how old the stone tool is?

The archaeologist could work out how old the bone is. The stone tool was buried next to it, so it'll be the same age.

"I understand how archaeologists and historians use sources, and why they must use them carefully."

Pupil Guidance:

"If they found a news article about a spaceship crash, would that prove that humans in 2014 had spaceships?" (Yes, with other supporting evidence.)

"What about if they found a video clip showing humans on spaceships, would that?" (Only if they could prove that it was not an entertainment programme, but a documentary about what was actually happening.)

Nearly always, the deeper something is buried in the ground, the older it is, but if there has been large-scale land movement (for example a massive tsunami or an earthquake) then sometimes layers get muddled. When this happens, radiocarbon dating of organic remains or comparison with artefacts from other sites may be needed to establish which layers are older.

More able pupils may mention that archaeologists can work out the age of the bone by looking at how many of a certain type of carbon atom are in it.

The First People in Britain

Stone Age to Celts: Activity Book p.6-7

By using computer imagery and analysis of these footprints, archaeologists think that there were probably five people in the group. There were bigger, heavier people, and smaller, lighter people. Their heights (which you can work out from the length of the stride) ranged from 1 m to 1.7 m. Could they have been a family? It's very possible. These are the earliest known human footprints outside Africa — an incredible find!

6

The First People in Britain

The earliest evidence we've found of people living in Britain comes from Happisburgh. The people who lived there were different to humans today. Look at pages 6 and 7 of the Study Book to find out about them.

This picture shows a stretch of sand at the Happisburgh site and some footprints that were found there.

Historians think they were made by a group of people walking in the muddy shore of the river.

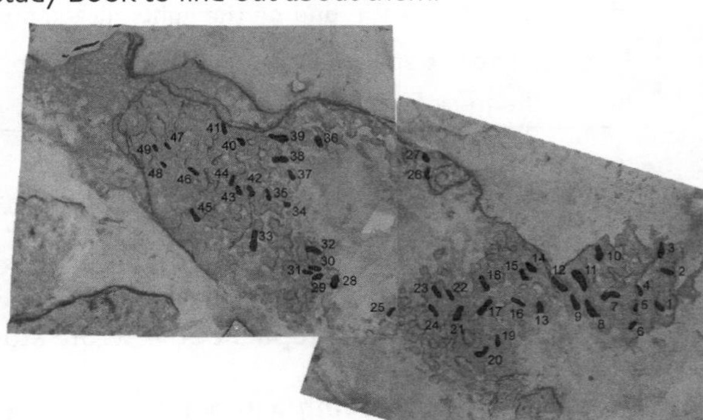

Write about daily life for the Happisburgh people. What do you think they were doing when the footsteps were made?

Use the picture and information in the Study Book to help you.

- *Gathering plants that they could eat.*
- *Hunting animals using stone and wooden tools.*
- *Washing in the river.*
- *Eating food by the river.*

Write down four differences between you and the Happisburgh people.

1) *The Happisburgh people had to hunt for their own*
2) *food. / They didn't wear clothes. / They didn't*
3) *cook their food. / They didn't live in houses. /*
4) *They lived alongside wild animals, etc.*

Pupil Guidance:

"*Imagine you were back in that time. What would your life be like? What dangers would you face?*"

Some of the differences pupils will say will be to do with material things — what was worn, eaten and made. Encourage pupils to go a little deeper than this. Would children have had any of the same dreams, or worries or fears? Would they have quarrelled with siblings, or played games?

Extension Idea

Pupils could think about the lives of primates today. Show them a video clip of young chimpanzees or gorillas playing, and think about similarities between their play and human play.

The First People in Britain: National Curriculum Aims

- Know the history of Britain as a chronological narrative.
- Understand similarity and difference and use them to draw contrasts.
- Create structured accounts.

7

List three things that you and the Happisburgh people have in common.

1) *Same number of arms and legs / live with other people*
2) */ need to eat to stay alive / walk on two legs / can use*
3) *tools / don't have fur / eat meat / have a family, etc.*

The Happisburgh people may have left Britain because of a glacial period.
Look at page 7 of the Study Book to find out what a glacial period was like.

Think of a place in Britain that you know well. In the box below, draw a picture of what it might have looked like in a glacial period.

Think how this place would have been different in the glacial periods. What would have been there? What wouldn't have been there?

This is .... *in the glacial periods.*

Write down two things that scientists have studied that have given them evidence that there were glacial periods.

1) • *ice cores*
2) • *cores from the sea bed*

"I know when the earliest evidence of people in Britain is from. I know what glacial periods are."

Pupils should show that it would be cold, e.g. by drawing ice or glaciers. They should recognise that there wouldn't be modern landmarks such as buildings. More able pupils may have included suggestions of what would have been there instead.

Suggested Scaffolding:

Give pupils a particular place to draw. E.g. the school fields, the local park.

Extension Idea

At the moment we are in an 'interglacial' period, but in the last million years there have been more than 10 major glacial periods. So things can — and do — change!

More able pupils could discuss what they know about the climate of Britain today and how it is changing.

More able pupils may mention that scientists study the remains of organisms in the sea bed cores.

Early Humans in Britain

Stone Age to Celts: Activity Book p.8-9

The scattered chips of flint from where the Boxgrove tool makers made their tools have been carefully re-assembled to form the shape of the flint core before it was made into a hand axe. Archaeologists can see exactly how the flint flakes were removed from the stone, and this helps them to see how the Boxgrove people worked their flint. They've tried to re-create the tools with modern flint, to help them understand the level of skill needed.

8

Early Humans in Britain

As the centuries went on, different groups of people lived in Britain. Their lives were very different to our lives today.

Read the Fact File below.

Boxgrove Fact File

Climate: cool, damp

Animals to hunt: deer, wild horse, rhinoceros, elephant

Animals that hunted people: lion, hyena

Cooking: No evidence of cooked food.

Clothes: No evidence of clothing.

Houses: Perhaps used caves as shelters. No settlements.

Tools: Made of stone.

Use the Fact File and page 8 of the Study Book to write about a day in the life of the Boxgrove people.

In the morning we *went to hunt some animals for food and to collect some water from the river.*

At lunch time we ate *the meat from the animals that we caught in the morning. Today it was deer.*

We were afraid of *animals like lions and hyenas. Hunting is sometimes scary because the animals can be very large.*

At night we slept in *a cave. If we hadn't found a nice cave we would have slept in the open air.*

Extension Idea

"How would you manage as a Stone Age person? Imagine that there are no shops, no money, and no way of obtaining anything you need — food, clean water, shelter — without making it or trading it yourself. What skills do you have that could help you?" (One reasonably large deer can provide a lot of what you need — skin for shelter, meat, sinew for tying things up, bones to turn into spears. But how do you kill the deer in the first place?)

Pupil Guidance:

"No evidence of clothing has been found. But can we say for certain that people didn't wear clothes at this time?"

Early Humans in Britain: National Curriculum Aims

- Know the history of Britain as a chronological narrative.
- Create structured accounts.
- Understand the methods of historical enquiry.
- Understand how evidence is used to make historical claims.

Scientists can tell a lot from a person's skeleton.

Read page 9 of the Study Book. Write down how scientists can tell whether a skeleton belonged to a man or a woman.

Some bones are different in men and women. For example, a man's skull is different from a woman's skull, and women have a larger pelvis.

Tick the two things below that scientists can tell from a skeleton.

- *What type of clothes the person wore.* ☐
- *If the person was male or female.* ☑
- *What time of day the person died.* ☐
- *How long ago the person lived.* ☑

Read about the Pontnewydd people on page 9 of the Study Book. If the Pontnewydd children came to your house today, what would amaze them?

Four things that they would be amazed by are:

1) *television / radio / doorbell / oven / the stairs /*
2) *windows / the fridge / the freezer / the washing*
3) *machine / all of the food in the house / the central*
4) *heating / that we have our own bedrooms, etc.*

"I can compare my life today with the lives of people who lived a long time ago."

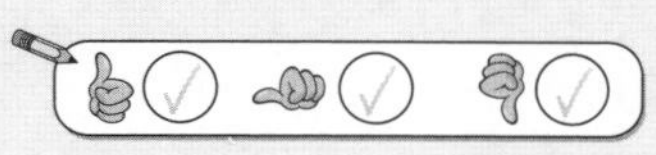

Other bones can tell us other things. Microscopic examination of the teeth from the Boxgrove site has shown that the enamel is covered in tiny nicks and scratches. This may be because teeth were used as tools. A hunter might cut meat by holding it in her teeth and then slicing a piece away from the carcass with her stone axe. She might use her teeth to steady a piece of wood before using both hands to chip away at it. Boxgrove teeth had a very hard time — they were used as tools, and it shows!

Extension Idea

"Do you think that the Pontnewydd children would be happy? Would they enjoy life as much as, less than or more than we do? Discuss!"

Pupil Guidance:

Encourage pupils to use the pictures in the Study Book not just to think about the negative aspects of living in the Stone Age, but the positive aspects. What dangers would they not have faced? Their air was clean, there were no wars, or bombs, or guns. There was probably very little fighting over resources, as there was so much to use for food, and so few people to eat it!

Life in the Glacial Periods

Stone Age to Celts: Activity Book p.10-11

It's important to remember that when we say that people 'lived in caves' they didn't live in caves in the same way that we live in houses. Shelter would have been temporary, and people would have moved around. This is because they would exhaust sources of food and materials if they stayed in the same place all the time. They would have to follow migratory herds, and their diet and forms of shelter would have been different at different times of the year.

Extension Idea

Pupils could discuss the significance of humans learning to make fire. They could list its uses, e.g. cooking, warmth, light, protection, comfort and its use as a focal point in gatherings of people.

10

Life in the Glacial Periods

Groups of people lived in Britain between glacial periods.

Compare the people in the picture below with the Happisburgh people on page 6 of the Study Book. Do you think these people or the Happisburgh people were more developed? Explain why.

I think that these *people were more developed because* they've learned how to make fire. This means they can cook food and keep themselves warm.

During the glacial periods, people across Europe were creating art.

Look at this example of cave art. What do you think it shows?

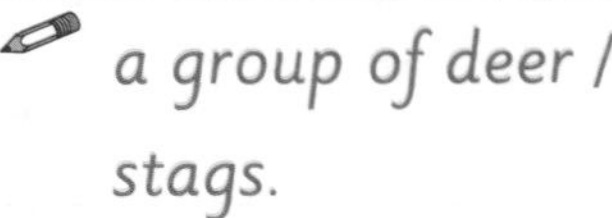

a group of deer / stags.

Some archaeologists believe that initially, art was thought to be a form of magic — by drawing the animal that you needed to kill for your food and clothing, you called it to you, and affirmed your ability to kill it and make yourself its conqueror.

Life in the Glacial Periods: National Curriculum Aims

- Know the history of Britain as a chronological narrative.
- Understand similarity and difference and use them to draw contrasts.
- Understand change.
- Understand how evidence is used to make historical claims.

Around 33 000 years ago, Paviland Man died.

Look at page 10 of the Study Book. What dangers might Paviland man have faced in his life? What dangers do you face in your life?

Dangers in Paviland Man's life:	Dangers in my life:
Getting hurt hunting animals / wild animals getting into his cave / not finding enough food, etc.	*Cars on busy roads / sharp objects / hot objects / fireworks / getting lost, etc.*

Tick the sentence below that you agree with. Explain why you agree with it.

Paviland Man's life was more dangerous than my life is. ☐

My life is more dangerous than Paviland Man's life was. ☐

I think this because ....

....

Archaeologists think that the people who lived in the Cheddar Caves were cannibals.

Look at page 11 of the Study Book. In your own words say why archaeologists think that these people were cannibals.

They found human bones that had marks made by stone knives and teeth on them. This made them think that people had eaten the meat off the bones.

"I know what life was like for people who lived in Britain between 50 000 and 11 500 years ago."

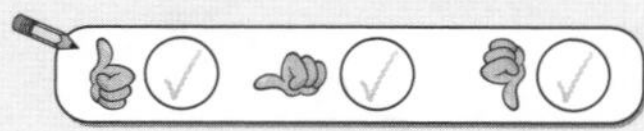

Like art, cannibalism may have been considered to be a form of magic. It is believed that throughout human history, one of the reasons that people have eaten other people is to share in their qualities — so if you killed a brave warrior and then ate part of him, you could share in the courage that he'd had.

Pupils may choose either sentence, as long as they support their decision with a good reason.

Suggested Scaffolding:

"Try and include these words in your answer:

- *bones*
- *knives*
- *teeth marks"*

Extension Idea

We may be disgusted by some Stone Age attitudes to things like cannibalism... but why? Is it because there is something absolutely wrong with them, or is it because we just find them unfamiliar? What would Stone Age people find disgusting about us?

The Mesolithic

Stone Age to Celts: Activity Book p.12-13

After the Mesolithic began there was no more glaciation. Remember that glaciation may have wiped out any evidence of early human habitation in the northern part of Britain. After 11 500 years ago there is far more evidence of human habitation from that area.

Extension Idea

Ask pupils to draw and label a diagram, or make a model of a Mesolithic hut.

The huts at Star Carr may not have been inhabited all the year round. Mesolithic humans were still semi-nomadic, although rather than wandering the land widely they may have shuttled between certain places. For example, a group of people may have camped by the seashore during the spring to make use of the protein from shellfish, other seafood, and sea-birds' eggs, and then moved to an area where they could find plants, fruit and nuts in the summer and autumn. They may then have holed up in semi-permanent shelters with all their stored food for the winter.

12

The Mesolithic

By 11 500 years ago, the glacial periods were over and the Mesolithic began. One of the earliest settlements in Britain during the Mesolithic was at Star Carr, in Yorkshire.

The picture below shows what the huts at Star Carr may have been like.

Look at the picture and read the description below.

Floor: earth and clay, covered with reeds.

Roof: wood, thatched with reeds, turf, hides or bark.

Lighting: none

Toilets and bathroom: none

What do you think it would have been like to live in a hut at Star Carr during the Mesolithic?

Write as much detail as you can about what you think it might have been like in the hut.

I think living in a hut at Star Carr would have been cold and drafty. It would have been uncomfortable to sit or sleep in as the floor would have been cold and hard. At night it would have been very dark because there was no lighting.

The people at Star Carr hunted animals for food. They used tools to hunt.

Draw a picture of one tool the Star Carr people might have used to hunt. What do you think the tool was made of? Use page 12 of the Study Book to help you.

This tool is made from deer antler / stone

Pupils should draw a spear or harpoon made from deer antler as shown on page 12 of the Study Book. Pupils could also draw a stone tool as these were used during the Mesolithic.

The Mesolithic: National Curriculum Aims

- Know the history of Britain as a chronological narrative.
- Create structured accounts.
- Understand how evidence is used to make historical claims.

Read pages 12 and 13 of the Study Book then tick the correct boxes to show whether the sentences below are true or false.

	True	False
There were lots of forests in Britain in the Mesolithic.	✓	
People didn't use stone tools in the Mesolithic.		✓
People ate deer, boar, fish, and beaver.	✓	
People used antler tools as well as stone tools.	✓	
People didn't travel around in the Mesolithic.		✓
Mesolithic people might have had spiritual beliefs.	✓	

Manu lived at Star Carr with his family.

Use pages 12 and 13 of your Study Book to write a short story about a day in Manu's life. Write about what he might have seen, done and eaten that day.

I went to the lake with my antler harpoon. I caught a few fish (no beaver today) and took them back to the hut for breakfast. After we'd eaten we headed to the forest and spent the rest of the day hunting for boar. My dad spotted an elk, but it saw us first and disappeared into the trees — what a shame! Once it started to get dark we headed back to the huts. We ate some boar and finished making our deer head dresses ready for tomorrow night's dancing.

"I can imagine what life was like for someone who lived around 11 500 years ago."

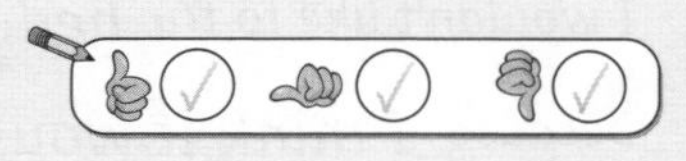

Extension Idea

Pupils could consider what skills are important at school (e.g. reading, writing and maths), and whether the same skills were important for people at Star Carr. Pupils could write a list of skills that they think would have helped them to survive in Mesolithic Britain.

Suggested Scaffolding:

"Try and include these words in your story:

- *hunting*
- *fish/deer/boar/elk*
- *hut*
- *antler head dress"*

Pupil Guidance:

"Remember that you will need to try and think about Manu's feelings as well as what he did for a great story!"

Extension Idea

Remind pupils that our views about different aspects of the Mesolithic may be very different from the views of someone alive at the time. For example, to Manu, the hut at Star Carr may have represented warmth, safety and shelter. Try a hot seating exercise to explore different interpretations.

Life in the Mesolithic

Stone Age to Celts: Activity Book p.14-15

Pupil Guidance:

"Write down all the different foods that you ate yesterday."

It's easy to think that Mesolithic people had a far more restricted diet than we do, but in many ways their diet was far more varied than ours. A large part of our diet comes from a small number of plants — wheat, rice and potatoes. Mesolithic humans would have eaten a massive range of plants. Some studies of pollen found in skeletons show that hundreds of different plants were eaten. Any meat would have been regarded as edible, and protein sources included many more species of seafood — such as limpets — than most people eat today.

14

Life in the Mesolithic

While Manu was living at Star Carr, other people were living in different parts of Britain, like Cheddar Gorge in Somerset. Their lives might have been quite similar to each others' lives, but they'd have been very different from your life...

Read p.14-15 of the Study Book to find out what Mesolithic people like Manu ate.

How would Manu's food have been different from yours?
Write a menu for one day's food for you, and a menu for one day for Manu.

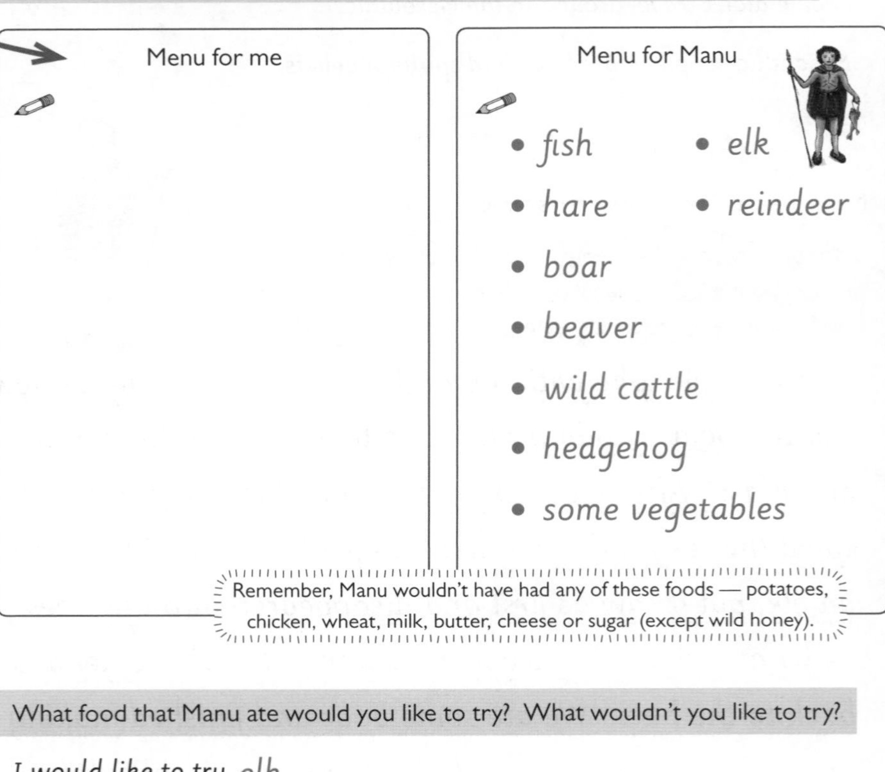

Menu for me

Menu for Manu

- fish
- hare
- boar
- beaver
- wild cattle
- hedgehog
- some vegetables
- elk
- reindeer

Remember, Manu wouldn't have had any of these foods — potatoes, chicken, wheat, milk, butter, cheese or sugar (except wild honey).

What food that Manu ate would you like to try? What wouldn't you like to try?

I would like to try elk

because I think it would be like beef, which I like.

I wouldn't like to try hedgehog

because I think it would be hard to get to the meat.

Extension Idea

Discuss the disadvantages of our food only coming from a few main sources.
What would happen if, suddenly, a disease wiped out every wheat crop in the world?
How would people feed themselves, and would they know how to find other food?

Life in the Mesolithic: National Curriculum Aims

- Know the history of Britain as a chronological narrative.
- Understand similarity and difference and use them to draw contrasts.

15

The picture below shows a cave in Cheddar Gorge.
People lived in the caves in Cheddar Gorge during the Mesolithic.

Circle the words below that describe what you think it would have been like to live in this cave.

Dark Wet Scary Safe Light Warm Cosy Exciting

Write one more word that describes what it would be like to live in this cave. *cold / damp / spooky*

A wide range of answers are possible, but the word written here should tie in with the adjectives chosen above.

Extension Idea
In pairs, get pupils to discuss with one another whether they would rather live in Mesolithic hut or in a cave.

Read page 15 of the Study Book. When people in the Mesolithic died, they were sometimes buried with things that they owned.

What do you think Manu would have owned? He wouldn't have had toys like yours, but what might he have had? Write or draw your answer.

I think Manu might have had spears and harpoons made of deer antler. He might have had a deer head dress and a necklace made of animal teeth.

Manu would have valued his clothes too – for example, a skin cloak and a pair of leather shoes.

"I can compare my life with the life of someone who lived around 11 500 years ago."

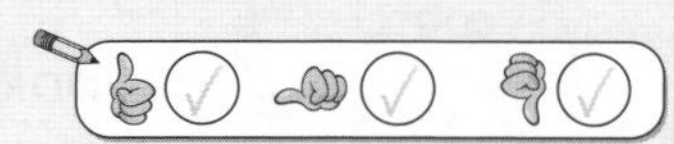

Extension Idea

Ask pupils to think about what Manu might have valued most. Ask them to imagine Manu going on a journey where he could only take a few things with him. What would he take? Then ask pupils to think about what they value. If they had to take only ten things on a long journey, what would they take?

Changes in the Mesolithic

Stone Age to Celts: Activity Book p.16-17

The Goldcliff area would have been very valuable to Mesolithic people. The wide mud flats, although dangerous (the Severn estuary has a huge tidal range, and fast-moving tides) would have provided large quantities of limpets, mussels, clams, and other seafood. Archaeological evidence shows that inland from the shore the reed beds and scrub were burned, perhaps to stop people travelling along the banks being ambushed by large predators!

Pupil Guidance:
"Have you ever been somewhere that looks like Goldcliff does in this picture? What did you do while you were there? What sorts of things did you see and hear?"

16

Changes in the Mesolithic

Archaeologists have found footprints on the coast at Goldcliff, in South Wales. They show that people walked there 7500 years ago.

This picture shows what Goldcliff looks like today.
Imagine going for a walk in Goldcliff today, then imagine going for a walk in Goldcliff 7500 years ago.

Look at page 16 of the Study Book to help you imagine Goldcliff 7500 years ago.

Complete the table below to say what both walks would be like.

	Today	7500 years ago
I would see...	*people having a picnic / joggers / parked cars*	*small wooden boats / huts / people fishing*
I would hear...	*boat engines / the waves / cars / people talking*	*people talking / the waves / birds / the wind*
Why might you be walking at the coast?	*to walk the dog / for exercise / to look at the views*	*to gather food / to get to a boat / to fish*

Pupil Guidance:
"Look at the picture on page 16 of the Study Book. What are the people in the picture doing? If you were there, what would you have seen and heard?"

Changes in the Mesolithic: National Curriculum Aims

- Know the history of Britain as a chronological narrative.
- Understand cause and consequence.
- Understand continuity, change and significance.
- Understand similarity and difference and use them to draw contrasts.

17

About 8200 years ago there was a tsunami in the North Sea.
Read page 17 of your Study Book then complete the sentences below.
Use the key words in the box to help you write the sentences.

Key Words: *wave* — *collapsed* — *layer of sand* — *island*

A tsunami is *a great wave.*

The tsunami happened because *a huge undersea shelf of rock off the coast of Norway suddenly collapsed.*

We know there was a tsunami because *a layer of sand was found in between layers of peat, 50 miles inland and four metres above the normal tide line in Scotland.*

After the tsunami, Britain *became an island.*

Imagine you were safe and watching the tsunami from a distance. What do you think you would have seen and heard? Write or draw your ideas in the box.

"I know that things change over time and that some changes can happen quickly and have a big effect."

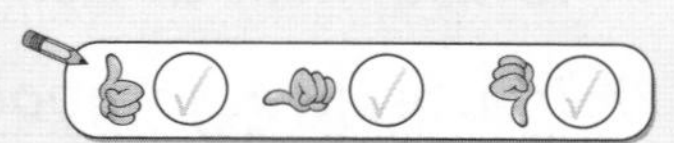

Doggerland is now Dogger Bank, a shallow area of the North Sea where fishermen fish for cod and haddock. When they draw their nets up, they sometimes find mammoth, hippopotamus, bison, and elk bones, as well as stone and bone tools, and sometimes even human remains.

Extension Idea

Pupils could discuss the significance of the tsunami in the history of Britain. How might life be different if Britain was still joined to the rest of Europe today?

Pupils' writing or drawing should show that they understand that the tsunami was a great wave which headed a long way inland.

Pupil Guidance:

"What noise would you expect such a great wave to make? What other sounds might you have been able to hear?"

Extension Idea

Sensitively edited footage of the 2004 tsunami could be used to explain exactly how devastating this wave might have been. Pupils could be encouraged to consider the similarities and differences between the two events — e.g. climate, landscape, types of settlements, and how many people may have been affected.

The Neolithic

Stone Age to Celts: Activity Book p.18-19

It's only with the advent of farming that permanent settlements arose. Until then most human communities had been completely or semi-nomadic. The agricultural lifestyle produced many social changes — differentiation in status, the concept of 'ownership' rather than 'stewardship' of land, and the development of war.

Agricultural lifestyles also meant that people had less food security. A nomadic group could move on and search elsewhere for food. The increase in static populations meant that if crops failed there would be famine. As the variety of edible plants eaten narrowed, people became more vulnerable to the failure of any of those edible plants.

Pupil Guidance:

"Domestication means breeding or training animals so that they're more useful to humans."

18

The Neolithic

After the Mesolithic came the Neolithic. Read pages 18-19 of the Study Book to find out the differences between life in the Mesolithic and life in the Neolithic.

For each sentence below, decide whether the person speaking lived during the Mesolithic or the Neolithic. If the speaker is Mesolithic colour the speech bubble in blue. If the speaker is Neolithic colour the speech bubble in red.

I move from place to place with my family. We never stay in the same place for long.

I own pottery jars of different sizes — they're really useful.

I have a cloak made from woven cloth.

All of my clothes are made from animal skins.

My family grows crops for food.

I live in a town with my family. We stay there all year round.

I hunt animals for food and I gather food wherever I can find it. I don't grow any food myself.

Why did Neolithic people domesticate animals? Give two reasons. Use page 18 of the Study Book to help you.

1) To use them as helpers.

2) To use them for food.

Extension Idea

Pupils could suggest how animals might have been used to help humans. What animals would have been the most useful?

The Neolithic: National Curriculum Aims

- Know the history of Britain as a chronological narrative.
- Understand similarity and difference and use them to draw contrasts.
- Understand continuity and change.

People started farming in the Neolithic.

Use page 19 of the Study Book to find out if these sentences about farming in the Neolithic are true or false. Tick the correct box for each statement.

	True	False
Farming started in Britain about 50 000 years ago.		✓
Some farmers may have come from abroad.	✓	
Some people caught diseases from the animals.	✓	
The more people there are, the more land is needed for farming.	✓	

The fist signs of farming in Britain are from about 6500 years ago.

In skeletons retrieved from early towns and villages there is evidence of more bone disease than in older skeletons. In older skeletons, there tends to be more bone trauma (for example, from a hunting wound).

Would you rather have been alive during the Mesolithic or the Neolithic? Why? You may want to use some of the words in the box in your answer.

farming *animals* *town* *fighting* *pottery* *disease*

These words are here to help you, but you don't need to use them all.

I would rather have been alive in the ....

because ....

....

....

....

....

....

In the Neolithic, life was more developed, but there was also fighting and disease. In the Mesolithic, life was less developed, but it was a more peaceful time.

"I know the differences between life in the Mesolithic and life in the Neolithic."

Extension Idea

Split pupils into small groups and assign half the groups as Mesolithic and half as Neolithic. Ask each group to come up with a short play showing what daily life was like for them. After the performances, discuss the differences with the class.

Neolithic Village Life

Stone Age to Celts: Activity Book p.20-21

A wide range of answers are possible, but pupils should focus on the differences between their day and Vali's day.

Extension Idea

Ask students if Vali would have been able to do some of the things they do every day. Encourage them to discuss why she would or wouldn't. For example, in the Neolithic there was no electricity, no modern technology, etc.

There is some debate as to what these objects actually are. Many archaeologists think they are weapons or were carried as a symbol of power. Some people think they may have been pieces of art. No-one knows for sure what they are, so a wide range of answers are possible.

20

Neolithic Village Life

Neolithic life was more settled than Mesolithic life. People didn't travel as much because they had to look after animals and crops.

"My name is Vali. I live at Skara Brae, in one of the stone houses."

Read pages 20 and 21 of the Study Book to find out what life was like at Skara Brae. Think about how this was different to how your life is.

What do you have to do each day?
How would Vali's day have been different?

Every day I have to have a shower, go to school, help set the table for dinner, walk the dog, and go to the shops with my mum.

Vali's day would be different because she might have had to go hunting or fishing, or feed the animals and help farm the crops.

Look at the picture below. These strange objects were found at Skara Brae. Archaeologists aren't sure what they are. What do you think they are?

Pupil Guidance:

"How do you think they could have been used? What do they look like? Do they remind you of anything?"

Neolithic Village Life: National Curriculum Aims

- Know the history of Britain as a chronological narrative.
- Understand similarity and difference and use them to draw contrasts.
- Understand how evidence is used to make historical claims.
- Understand why there are different interpretations of the past.

21

On page 20 of the Study Book there's a photograph of the remains of a house at Skara Brae.

Draw and label a picture of what you think the inside of the house looked like when Vali was alive. Use the photograph and other information on the page to help you.

Pupil Guidance:

"Look at the ruins in the photograph. Imagine what each part of the house would have looked like when it was new. What would the stone dresser have looked like? What would the hearth have looked like?"

Pupils' drawings should show a house made from flat rocks. The roof should be made of turf and wood and have a smoke hole. There shouldn't be any windows. The inside of the building should show a central hearth, a stone dresser, beds and a tank for fish bait.
More able pupils might also draw objects belonging to the Neolithic people, such as woven cloth, pottery, tools, etc.

Look at the pictures below. Do you think picture A or picture B shows Neolithic tools? Why do you think this? Use page 21 of the Study Book to help you.

Picture A *shows Neolithic tools.*

I can tell because they look smooth and I know that people in the Neolithic ground and polished their tools.

Suggested Scaffolding:

"Use these words in your answer:

- *smooth*
- *polished"*

"I know about daily life during the Neolithic."

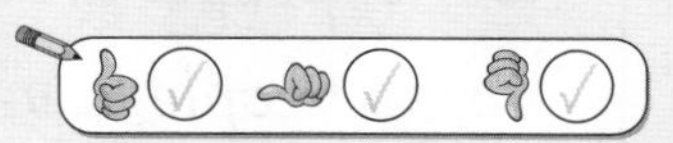

It would have taken a long time for someone to carefully shape, smooth and polish those stones. The community where they lived must have been able to support them with food while they were making them. For every person occupied in making an object like this, someone else had to be able to provide them with food.

Neolithic Stone Circles

Stone Age to Celts: Activity Book p.22-23

Pupil Guidance:
"What had the Neolithic people started doing that the Mesolithic people hadn't done? Why would knowing when the seasons were be useful to Neolithic people?"

Extension Idea
In the playground, draw one of the stones to scale using chalk, so that pupils can see how big the stones actually are.

Extension Idea
The stones at Stonehenge may have been transported on rollers. Pupils could model this method using books or bricks to represent the stones, and pencils or other cylindrical objects as rollers.

Pupil Guidance:
"How big are the stones? How are they arranged? What would you have thought of them?"

22

Neolithic Stone Circles

Historians think people began to keep track of time, like the changing seasons, during the Neolithic. Stone circles may have been built to help them do this.

Why was it important to know when the seasons would change in the Neolithic? Circle the correct answer below. Use page 22 of the Study Book to help you.

So you knew when Christmas was.

So you knew what clothes you needed.

So you knew when to plant and harvest crops.

Stonehenge is a Neolithic stone circle. Neolithic people travelled long distances to visit Stonehenge.

Some of the stones are over 6 metres tall — that's 4 times taller than an average woman.

Imagine you were a visitor to Stonehenge in Neolithic times.
Write a description of what it would have been like.
Use pages 22 and 23 of the Study Book and the picture above to help you.

The stones are huge — they're the biggest thing I've ever seen in my life! Some are just by themselves, but there are others with stones laid on top of them. I don't know how they got them up there! There are lots of people around — the summer solstice is coming up, so people have been arriving from all over.

Recent geophysical examinations of the site around Stonehenge has shown that it does not sit alone in its landscape as it appears to. It was part of a complex of sites that existed long before the first stone circles were built, with the first evidence of human manipulation of the landscape now dating back to 8000 BC in the Mesolithic.

Neolithic Stone Circles: National Curriculum Aims

- Know the history of Britain as a chronological narrative.
- Create structured accounts.
- Understand how evidence is used to make historical claims.

Draw a circle around the sentences below that you think are correct.
Use pages 22 and 23 of the Study Book if you need help.

Durrington Walls was a village near Stonehenge.

The winter and summer solstices were important days to Neolithic people.

The longest day of the year is the winter solstice.

Stonehenge wasn't in Britain.

Knowing when the summer and winter solstices were was important for farming.

Archaeologists have found evidence that some Neolithic people celebrated the winter solstice with a feast near Stonehenge.

Imagine you travelled back in time to the winter solstice 4500 years ago.
Write or draw what you might have seen happening.

"I know that Neolithic people built stone circles and understand some reasons why they built them."

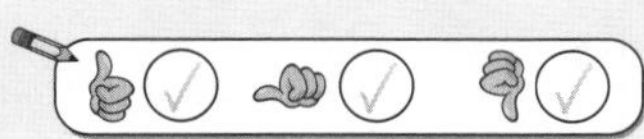

We don't know the details of how Neolithic people celebrated the winter solstice, so a wide range of answers are possible here. Pupils should be encouraged to use their imaginations.

Pupil Guidance:
"What do you think the weather would have been like at the winter solstice? What would people have been wearing? What do you think they'd be eating?"

Extension Idea
Stonehenge is now a popular tourist attraction. Pupils could make a leaflet advertising Stonehenge. They could include pictures and details of the history of Stonehenge. More able pupils could find further information on Stonehenge using books or the Internet.

Flint, Copper and Bronze

Stone Age to Celts: Activity Book p.24-25

Pupil Guidance:

"Think about what equipment miners in the Neolithic might have had compared to the equipment that miners have today. What equipment do miners today have that helps to keep them safe? Would miners in the Neolithic have had this equipment?

Do you think the pits were stable in the Neolithic or were they likely to collapse? What about today?"

Grime's Graves is an example of a Neolithic flint mine. Evidence suggests that the smallest tunnels were mined by women and children. Two girls' skeletons have been found, suggesting that mining was a dangerous job.

Pupil Guidance:

Pupils may need further guidance as to what modern underground mining is like. For example, in many modern mines the ceilings are supported using metal bolts, the mines are ventilated, and lifts are used to transport miners, materials and machinery in and out of the mines.

24

Flint, Copper and Bronze

In the Neolithic, people mined flint to make tools from. People still mine for things these days. The picture below shows some people down a mine today.

Look at this picture.
Now read about Neolithic mining and look at the picture of the mine on page 24 of your Study Book.

Do you think mining is more or less dangerous today, than it was in the Neolithic? Explain your answer.

I think that mining in the Neolithic was *more dangerous because* the miners didn't have hard hats like they do today, or electric lights to help them see. The mines were more likely to collapse because the equipment they used to dig and support the sides of the mine wasn't as good.

Historians think that children would have been sent down the mines because they could get into the smallest tunnels.

Look at page 24 of the Study Book. Imagine you worked down the mines. In the box below write or draw what you think it would have been like.

Pupil Guidance:

"Would it have been cold? Would there be much light? Would you have felt scared? Why?"

Flint, Copper and Bronze: National Curriculum Aims

- Know the history of Britain as a chronological narrative.
- Know how people's lives have shaped Britain.
- Understand similarity and difference and use them to draw contrasts.

At the end of the Neolithic, people in Britain started to make tools and weapons out of copper.

Read page 25 of your Study Book then tick the correct boxes to show whether the sentences below are true or false.

	True	False
People in Britain made tools out of copper 20 000 years ago.	☐	☑
People who made copper tools could swap them for things that they needed.	☑	☐
Copper is a type of rock.	☐	☑
The Stone Age ended when people started making tools from metal.	☑	☐
You need to melt copper to shape it into tools and weapons.	☑	☐
The people of Britain were the first people to discover how to make tools out of copper.	☐	☑

People in Britain started making tools out of copper around 4500 years ago.

Copper ore is rock that copper (a metal) is extracted from.

Copper tools were made and used in mainland Europe before they were made in Britain.

The Bronze Age in Britain started about 4000 years ago. It's when people started to make things out of bronze. Look at page 25 of the Study Book.

What is bronze a mixture of? Tick two boxes.

flint	☐	*copper*	☑
gold	☐	*tin*	☑

Why did people start to make things out of bronze instead of copper?

People started making things out of bronze because it was harder and stronger than copper.

"I know about flint mining and I understand how the use of copper and bronze developed."

Although people in this period chose between materials such as copper, bronze, bone and stone for their suitability for different uses, aesthetic considerations were also important. The extreme effort needed to decorate dagger hilts with minute pieces of gold wire, for example, shows that people didn't just want something that was useful. They also wanted something that was beautiful and valuable.

Life After the Stone Age

Stone Age to Celts: Activity Book p.26-27

All the evidence points to Stonehenge as being a place of pilgrimage — an area where people derived a spiritual meaning from the landscape, the objects in the landscape, and possibly the rituals and work that went on there.

26

Life After the Stone Age

Some of the remains found near Stonehenge tell us that people travelled — people who were alive just after the Stone Age came from all over Europe to visit Stonehenge.

Why do you think people travelled to Stonehenge from different countries? Why do people travel to different countries today?

People travelled to Stonehenge because they thought it was an important place. / they wanted to celebrate the summer and winter solstices.

Today people travel to different countries to go on holiday, visit their families or go on business trips.

Pupils' answers could be compiled to see how many different reasons the class can come up with for why people travelled to Stonehenge and why people travel abroad today.

Read about the Boscombe Bowmen on page 27 of the Study Book.

Where do archaeologists think the Boscombe Bowmen came from?

Archaeologists think they came from Wales .

In the box on the right, draw one of the things found in the grave that gave the Boscombe Bowmen their name. What do you think this object was made of?

The thing I've drawn is made of: flint / bone

Pupils should draw a picture showing an arrowhead found in the grave of the Boscombe Bowmen. These arrowheads were actually made of flint, but pupils may have chosen flint or bone for their answer.

Life After the Stone Age: National Curriculum Aims

- Know the history of Britain as a chronological narrative.
- Create structured accounts.
- Understand how evidence is used to make historical claims.

27

Read about the Amesbury Archer and his companion on pages 26 and 27 of the Study Book.

Draw a picture of what you think the Archer would have looked like in the box below. Then, imagine that you are the Archer telling someone the story of your life. Write down what you would say to them.

I am the Archer. I was born in the Alps, but I travelled to Britain to see Stonehenge. It was a very long journey, but it was worth it. I lived with my family for many years here. I was a very good archer, so I always carried my bow and lots of spare arrows with me.

For your pictures, think about what they might have worn and carried with them.

Now do the same for the companion...

I am the companion. I was raised in the south of England near Stonehenge. I spent lots of time with my family here when I was younger, but I decided to travel further north when I was a teenager.

"I know that people who were alive just after the Stone Age travelled to places that were important to them."

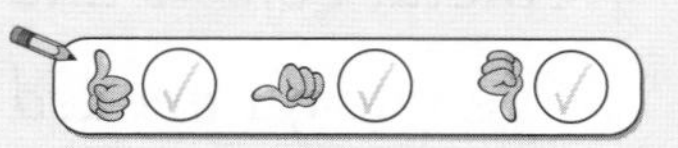

Pupil Guidance:

"Where was the archer born? Where did he travel to during his life? Do you think he had any family?"

Scientists believe that the Archer came from central Europe because they have conducted oxygen isotope analysis of the enamel in his teeth. In this analysis technique, the ratio of different oxygen isotopes in teeth is compared to the ratio in drinking water from different regions, so scientists can tell where the person may have lived when their teeth were formed.

Pupil Guidance:

"Do you think the archer and the companion knew each other? You might want to include this in your story."

Pupils might include details in their drawings such as the gold hair ornaments, the copper knives and a bow and arrows.

Extension Idea

Ask pupils to think of a (long-ish) journey they have taken recently. How did they travel? How much did they see or notice on their journey? Did they interact with people on the way? Then ask them to imagine doing the same journey on foot. How would their experience have been different?

Bronze Age Travel and Trade

Stone Age to Celts: Activity Book p.28-29

The Neolithic saw the first real status distinctions in human society: the difference between who 'owned' land and animals, and who didn't. You would derive status from what you had, how much food you could produce, store, and distribute, and, ultimately, how many workers on your land relied on you for their food (and could then be persuaded to fight for you). These distinctions deepened in the Bronze Age, and a different class of people emerged. You could become rich either by owning and trading goods worked from metal, or by possessing the knowledge to work the metal and produce these goods.

28

Bronze Age Travel and Trade

In the Bronze Age there was a difference between the rich and the poor.

For each speech bubble below, decide whether the Bronze Age person speaking is more likely to be rich or poor. Write your answer under each speech bubble.

I trade metals for a living.

rich

Use pages 28-29 of the Study Book to help you if you get stuck.

I am good at working metals such as bronze and gold.

rich

I don't own anything worth trading.

poor

I don't own any bronze.

poor

I wear a gold armlet to show my importance.

rich

Look at the cape on page 29 of your Study Book.

Imagine you were the person who owned it. What do you think your life would have been like? Do you think you lived well? Write your ideas in the box below.

I was a very important person in my village — I wore my cape to show my importance. I owned lots of metal objects and so I had lots of things to trade with people if I needed anything. My life was good.

Extension Idea

The gold cape is called the Mold cape and was discovered in 1833 by some men working in a quarry in Mold in North Wales. Ask pupils to write a newspaper article reporting the discovery.

Pupil Guidance:

"Look at what the cape is made of.
What clues does this give you as to what your life would have been like?"

Bronze Age Travel and Trade: National Curriculum Aims

- Know the history of Britain as a chronological narrative.
- Understand similarity and difference and use them to draw contrasts.
- Understand how evidence is used to make historical claims.

29

The picture below shows men farming the land.

Look at the picture of the men on page 28 of your Study Book. Which men do you think were richer? Explain your answer.

I think that the men working the metal *were richer because* they would have been able to make things that they could trade.

Read page 29 of your Study Book.

Read the sentences below. Circle the ones that you think are true.

Archaeologists think the amber necklace was from Wales.

Archaeologists sometimes use people's teeth to work out where they were from.

People from abroad brought new ways of working metal to Britain.

Archaeologists think the boy with the amber necklace was from Stonehenge.

"I know that in the Bronze Age some people were rich and some were poor and I understand why."

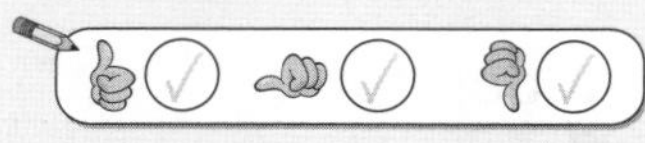

Extension Idea

Ask pupils to imagine they were a Bronze Age metal worker, possessing the secret of shaping this amazing new metal. Would they share their secret? Discuss as a class, making sure pupils give reasons for whatever decision they come to.

The beads that make the amber necklace are thought to have come from Scandinavia. The boy the necklace was buried with is believed to be from the Mediterranean.

Extension Idea

Inequality is something that offends a lot of people. Ask pupils whether they think it is possible to have a society where everyone has the same amount of money and belongings? If yes, how would they go about achieving it? Debate the issue in class and think about your conclusions.

Life in the Bronze Age

Stone Age to Celts: Activity Book p.30-31

Initially horses were hunted as food. No one knows exactly when people decided that it would be a good idea to ride them or use them to draw wheeled vehicles. The first archaeological evidence of horses buried with chariots was found in modern-day Russia, and dates from about 4000 years ago. However, the first evidence of horses being domesticated and living with humans is from at least 1500 years before that.

The horse is one of the major factors in driving population expansion and warfare in the Bronze Age. Cultures that had and used horses had a powerful means of getting around. They could use horse power to transport, not just themselves, but also trade-goods and armies.

30

Life in the Bronze Age

In the Bronze Age, people travelled on foot and by boat. Some historians think that they might have begun to use horses to travel around too.

Give two ways that humans might have used horses for travelling in the Bronze Age.

1) *They could have ridden horses to travel about.*

2) *They could have had carts pulled by horses to carry their belongings around in.*

Think about how humans could have used horses to get around, and how they could have used horses to move their things around.

Dhu lived at Must Farm in the Fens. Read what he has to say.

"I live with my family in a hut. My father is a bronzesmith. I help look after our animals and crops. My mother weaves our clothes out of wool."

Use pages 30-31 of the Study Book to help you answer these questions.

What do you think Dhu's sword and shield are made of? Tick the box.

iron ☐ stone ☐ bronze 

What do you think Dhu's mother uses to weave clothes?

A loom.

Extension Idea

Pupils could make 'looms' by cutting evenly spaced slits into the shorter ends of a shoebox and tying loops of string around the shoebox, one loop in each slit. They could then use thin strips of different coloured fabrics to weave the material over and under the strings.

Life in the Bronze Age: National Curriculum Aims

- Know the history of Britain as a chronological narrative.
- Understand similarity and difference and use them to draw contrasts.
- Understand change.

31

Life had changed a lot in the 8000 years since the Mesolithic began. Look back at what you wrote about Manu's life in the Mesolithic on pages 12-15 of this book.

In the box below, write how Manu's life was different from Dhu's. Think about things like what they both wore, what they ate and what they would have spent their days doing. Use pages 30-31 of the Study Book to help you.

Pupils could also look at pages 12-15 of the Study Book if they want more information about life in the Mesolithic.

Manu's life	Dhu's life
• *tools and weapons made of stone or antler* • *hunted and gathered food* • *ate food such as fish, vegetables and meats including boar and elk* • *no woven clothes*	• *weapons made of bronze* • *farmed crops* • *kept animals* • *ate food such as grain, fish and eel* • *woven clothes* 

Suggested Scaffolding:

- "Manu ate..."
- "Dhu wore..."
- "Each day Manu would have..."

Would you rather have lived as Manu did or as Dhu lived? Explain why.

I would rather have lived like .... *because* ....

....

....

....

Pupils should give their own opinion, and justify it with a reason relating to their response to the above question.

"I know what daily life was like in the Bronze Age and I know how people travelled."

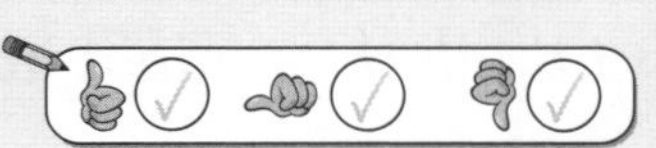

Extension Idea

Pupils could compare their lives now with the lives of Manu from the Mesolithic and Dhu from the Bronze Age.

The End of the Bronze Age

Stone Age to Celts: Activity Book p.32-33

Pupils' answers should show that the weather was cold and wet. More able pupils might talk about the risk of flooding.

Extension Idea

People at this time were living in huts. Ask pupils to consider what it would be like living in a hut when the weather was like this.

Pupils' drawings should show Bronze Age people throwing metal goods such as swords, shields and axes into rivers or streams.

Suggested Scaffolding:

"I think they might have found..."

32

The End of the Bronze Age

By the end of the Bronze Age, the weather in Britain had changed a lot.
Read page 32 of your Study Book.

Imagine you are living in Britain towards the end of the Bronze Age. Write a weather forecast describing what the weather will be like for the next three days.

Today will be chilly with heavy rain all day. Tomorrow, there will be thunder and lightning for most of the day, followed by heavy rain and high winds the day after.

Archaeologists believe that Bronze Age people made offerings to the water spirits and gods. Read page 32 of your Study Book. In the box below draw a picture of people making offerings. Label your drawing to explain what it shows.

What evidence do you think archaeologists have for thinking that people made offerings to water spirits?

Hint: What do you think they might have found?

I think they might have found weapons like bronze swords and axes in rivers and streams.

The reason we believe that Bronze Age people may have made offerings to try to stop the bad weather is because there is evidence that their religion was animistic — they assigned souls or spirits to important things, such as fire, the Sun or a river. Offering their most precious belongings to these things was their way of trying to make the spirits be kind to them once more.

The End of the Bronze Age: National Curriculum Aims

- Know the history of Britain as a chronological narrative.
- Understand cause and consequence.
- Understand how evidence is used to make historical claims.
- Understand change.

People began to farm in hillforts towards the end of the Bronze Age.

Use page 33 of the Study Book to help you draw a hillfort. Label the different parts of your picture to show what they are and what they are made from.

Pupils' drawings should show a fort on top of a hill. The top of the hill should be surrounded by a wall made of earth, wood or stone. There should be buildings and farming taking place within the hillfort. The different features of the hillfort should be labelled.

Towards the end of the Bronze Age, people started making alliances and living in tribes. Read pages 32 and 33 of your Study Book.

Think about what advantages this would have given people over just living with their families.

Why do you think people started doing this?

I think people started making alliances and living in tribes because if you lived in a tribe there were more people to protect you and defend your land if you were attacked.

Another advantage was sharing responsibilty for work, such as growing food, hunting and making weapons. When times were hard and there was not much food, being in a big tribe might also mean that you were powerful enough to take what you needed from other smaller tribes.

One disadvantage was that you needed so much more food to support all of those people.

"I know what life was like in Britain towards the end of the Bronze Age."

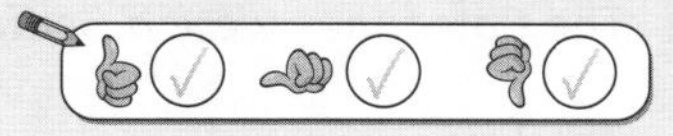

Extension Idea

Ask pupils to imagine that they are the leader of a small clan and get them to write a speech persuading their people to join a larger, more powerful tribe.

The Celtic Age of Iron

The Celtic Age of Iron: Activity Book p.34-35

34

The Celtic Age of Iron

Historians think that people in Britain first started using iron about 2700 years ago. Read page 34 of your Study Book.

Why might people have started using iron instead of bronze?

There was a shortage of bronze. / They might have found ways of making better, cheaper, stronger items from iron.

Iron gradually rusts away when it comes into contact with air and water. The sickle and sword found at Llyn Fawr are from about 2700 years ago — they are some of the earliest examples of iron found in Britain.

Do you think people in Britain used iron before 2700 years ago? Tick the sentence below that you agree with. Explain why you agree with it.

People in Britain definitely didn't use iron before 2700 years ago. ☐

People in Britain definitely used iron before 2700 years ago. ☐

People in Britain could have used iron before 2700 years ago. ☑

I think this because *there might have been iron, but it might not have been found yet, or it could have rusted away.*

Extension Idea

Display rusting to pupils by placing a nail in a jar of water. Leave the nail for a few days until rust begins to form. Pupils could also be shown pictures of objects rusting away over time.

People living in the Iron Age are often known as Celts.

Read page 35 of your Study Book. Tick the correct boxes to show whether the sentences below are true or false.

	True	False
There were no Celtic tribes outside of Britain.	☐	☑
The Celts were made up of lots of different tribes.	☑	☐
The Caledones were a Celtic tribe from Scotland.	☑	☐
The Iceni are an example of a Celtic tribe.	☑	☐

'Celtic' is not a racial designation. It refers to people who speak common or related languages, and have a similar lifestyle and culture. So tribes may share a 'Celtic' culture, but they are not a 'race' or a single group of people.

The Celtic Age of Iron: National Curriculum Aims

- Know the history of Britain as a chronological narrative.
- Understand cause and consequence.
- Understand how evidence is used to make historical claims.
- Understand similarity and difference and use them to draw contrasts.

35

Look at the map showing where the Celtic tribes lived on page 35 of your Study Book.

Which of these tribes lived closest to where you live?

The tribe that lived closest to me is the .... tribe.

Pupils should use the map on page 35 of the Study Book to name the Celtic tribe that lived closest to them.

Look at the picture of the Iron Age family on page 35 of your Study Book.

In the boxes below, describe the differences between an Iron Age family and your family. Think about where they live. Look at the things they're doing. What different things do you and your family do when you're at home?

Iron Age Family	My Family
They live in a hut. / They cook their food on a fire in the middle of the room. / They all live in one room. / They spend their time talking and doing jobs. / Their floor is made of earth, etc.	*I live in a house. / We cook our food in an oven in the kitchen. / We have our own bedrooms. / We watch TV and play games. / Our floors are covered with carpets, etc.*

Suggested Scaffolding:

"Include some of these words in your answer:

- *hut*
- *cook*
- *bedroom*
- *kitchen*
- *television*
- *fire*
- *carpet*
- *clothes"*

Are there any similarities between your family and the Iron Age family? List as many as you can.

Their mum cooks the food and so does my mum. The children look like they are helping their mum cook and I help my mum cook.

"I know about the use of iron in the Iron Age, and I know who the Celts were."

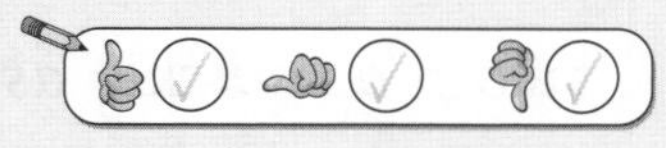

Extension Idea

Get pupils to find out a little more about how iron is made, and write an imaginative diary entry as if they were seeing a blacksmith make an iron sword for the first time.

Life in the Iron Age

Stone Age to Celts: Activity Book p.36-37

The Iron Age was a time when small groups of people coalesced into tribes, and began to develop tribal alliances and have wars. The reasons for this were various, but it is significant that many Celtic, Welsh and Gaelic stories from this period stress the importance of leaders as ring and gift givers, but also as providers of huge feasts for their followers. In a worsening climate, with a rising population, the most respected leaders were no longer those who could give many bronze axes, but those who could provide large numbers of people with food security.

36

Life in the Iron Age

Danebury Hillfort was an Iron Age hillfort.
Fifion lives at Danebury Hillfort. Read what she has to say.

"I live and work with my family in the hillfort. We are kept busy with the farming. Life is good, but we worry about being attacked by other tribes."

In the box below, write a story set in Danebury Hillfort. Make Fifion the main character in your story. Try and make your story as descriptive and exciting as you can. Use pages 36 and 37 of the Study Book to help you.

Fifion staggered slowly back to the hut. She was struggling with the milk she was carrying. It was sloshing all over the place, but she needed to hurry — her mother would be angry if she was late back to help prepare the food. Suddenly Fifion heard a loud cry from one of her tribe up near the wall.

"ATTACK! TO THE GATE! THEY'RE COMING!"

Fifion dropped the milk in a panic and scrambled to the wall of the hillfort to see for herself. Yes, it was true. A large group of vicious looking men were heading straight towards the hill. The day she feared had come. She turned and fled to the hut — she needed to get her sword as quickly as possible to help defend their land.

Suggested Scaffolding:

"In your story you could include:

- *What Fifion was doing that day.*
- *An attack on the hillfort by another tribe.*
- *How Fifion reacted to the attack."*

Suggested Scaffolding:

"Include these words in your story: hillfort – tribe – attack – sword – run – fight."

Life in the Iron Age: National Curriculum Aims

- Know the history of Britain as a chronological narrative.
- Create structured accounts.
- Understand how evidence is used to make historical claims.

What evidence of fighting have archaeologists found at Danebury Hillfort? Use page 37 of your Study Book to help you.

Archaeologists have found some damaged skulls and evidence of burial pits.

The picture below shows the remains of a hillfort.

Do you think a hillfort would be easy or hard to attack? Why?

I think a hillfort would be hard *to attack because* the sides of the hillfort were steep, so they would be difficult to climb while carrying weapons and being attacked from above.

Look at the sword on page 37 of the Study Book.

Draw what you think the sword would have looked like when it was new. Write four words that would have described the sword when it was new.

1) shiny
2) sharp
3) heavy
4) dazzling

"I know that life in Britain was sometimes peaceful and sometimes violent during the Iron Age."

Extension Idea

Pupils could research and study any Iron Age settlements or hillforts in the local area. Hillfort remains are most common in the south and south-west of England, the coasts of Scotland and Wales, and along the Welsh-English border.

A wide range of answers are possible. Pupils need to justify their answer with a reason.

Extension Idea

Ask pupils to design and make their own Iron Age weapon, or make a replica of the sword on page 37 of the Study Book. They could construct their weapon using papier mâché and decorate it using tissue paper, foil, etc.

We know from some of the written narratives of Romans and others visiting Britain that by this time the Britons had the reputation of being fierce warriors. They bred shaggy, strong little native ponies, and harnessed these to chariots which they drove with incredible skill. Warriors went into battle bare-chested and regarded wearing armour as cowardly!

An Invasion from Rome

Stone Age to Celts: Activity Book p.38-39

Rome was founded in 753 BC, and the Roman Empire steadily expanded over the next seven hundred years. The advantage the Romans had was their army: it was composed of professional soldiers, who signed on for a twenty-year length of duty. The Romans saw conquest as innate to their nature — and they believed that their version of 'civilisation' was the way forward for everyone. In the case of their invasion of Britain, their motto was 'my enemy's friend is also my enemy'; they were not prepared to tolerate the Gauls being aided from Britain.

Pupils could also have written that Julius Caesar wanted to invade Britain for the glory of conquering new lands.

Pupil Guidance:

"History began when prehistory ended. Have a look at pages 2-3 of the Study Book to find out the difference between history and prehistory."

38

An Invasion from Rome

Life in Britain changed a lot when the Romans arrived.

Read page 38 of your Study Book, then fill in the gaps in the sentences below.

The city of Rome is in Italy. *By about 2250 years ago, the Romans were starting to build an* empire. *Around 2060 years ago, a Roman leader called* Julius Caesar *tried to conquer Gaul completely.*

Have a look at pages 38 and 39 of your Study Book.

Give two reasons why Julius Caesar wanted to invade Britain.

1) To stop the tribes in Britain helping the people in Gaul fight the Romans.

2) To get metals such as gold, silver, lead, copper and tin.

Read the sentence below.

"History began in Britain when the Romans arrived."

Read page 39 of your Study Book.
Tick the sentence below that explains why the sentence above is true.

Exciting things started happening once the Romans came to Britain. ☐

It's when BC and AD dating was first used in Britain. ☐

It's when people in Britain started writing things down. ☑

An Invasion from Rome: National Curriculum Aims

- Know the history of Britain as a chronological narrative.
- Know and understand significant aspects of the history of the wider world, for example, the expansion of empires.
- Know and use historical terms such as 'empire', 'AD' and 'BC'.

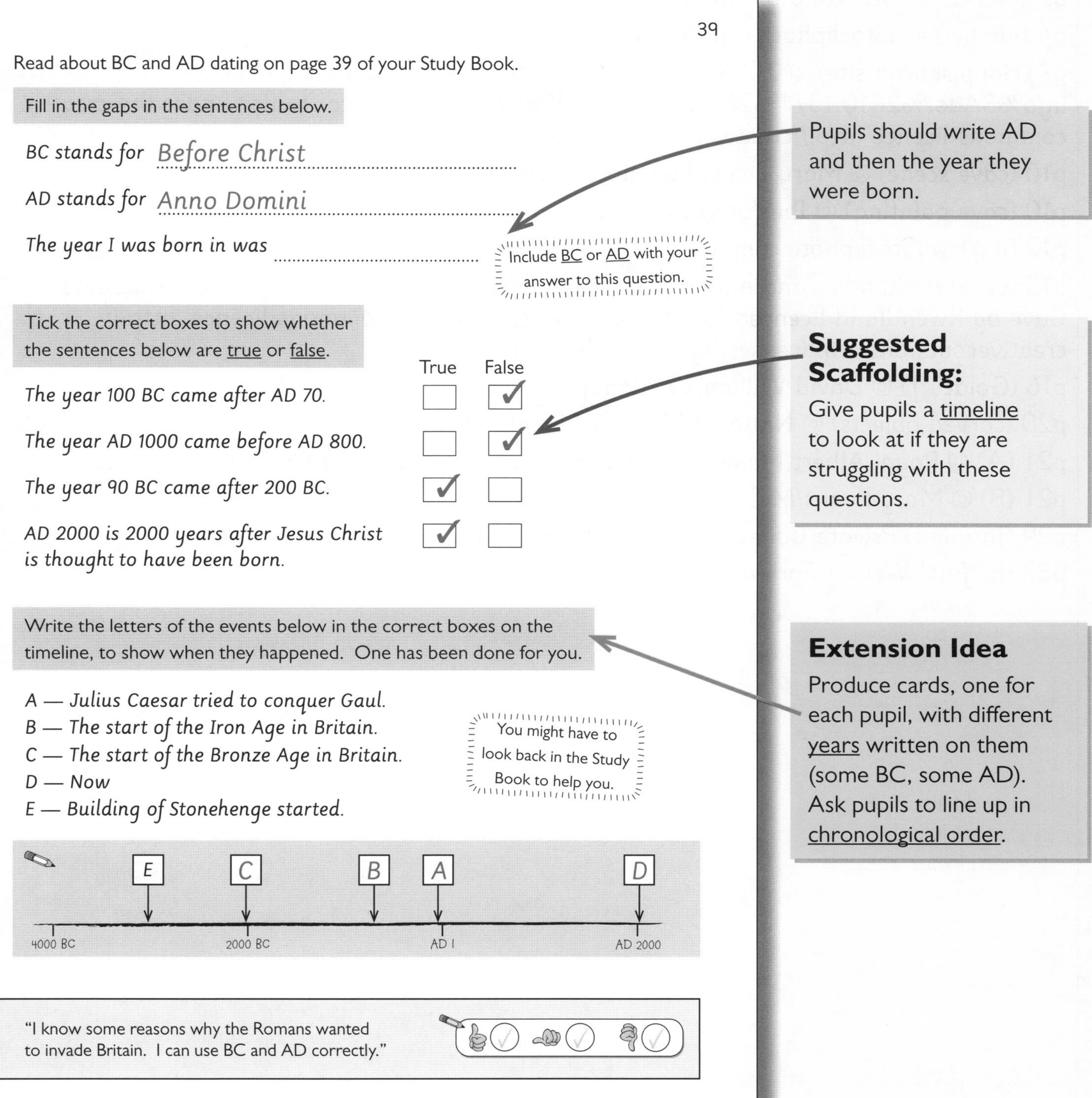

Pupils should write AD and then the year they were born.

Suggested Scaffolding:
Give pupils a timeline to look at if they are struggling with these questions.

Extension Idea

Produce cards, one for each pupil, with different years written on them (some BC, some AD). Ask pupils to line up in chronological order.

Extension Idea

As a class, create a timeline for the events in this book, and decorate it with details of what happened when. Ask more able pupils whether it would be possible to draw the entire timeline to scale. (N.B. If one year on this timeline were represented by 1 cm, the timeline would be about 9500 m long!)

Picture acknowledgements

Thumb illustration used throughout the book © iStockphoto.com
p2 (tool A) © iStockphoto.com/MarVal.
p2 (tool B) © iStockphoto.com/lucamanieri.
p2 (tool C) © iStockphoto.com/Laurentius.
p4 (jumper) © iStockphoto.com/mattjeacock.
p7 (Happisburgh site) © 2014 Ashton et al. http://www.plosone.org/article/info%3Adoi%2F10.1371%2Fjournal.pone.0088329 licenced for re-use under the creative commons licence http://creativecommons.org/licenses/by/4.0/.
p10 (cave scene) © Mary Evans/Fonollosa/Iberfoto.
p10 (cave painting) © Iberfoto/Mary Evans.
p12 (hut) © iStockphoto.com/TT.
p15 (cave) A chamber and mirror pool inside Gough's Cave, Cheddar, called Alladdin's Cave by Rwendland licenced for re-use under the creative commons licence, http://creativecommons.org/licenses/by-sa/3.0/deed.en.
p16 (Goldcliff) © David Williams / Alamy.
p20 (carved objects) © National Museums Scotland.
p21 (A) © Royal Albert Memorial Museum, Exeter, Devon, UK / Bridgeman Images.
p21 (B) © Mary Evans/M.C.Esteban/Iberfoto.
p29 (farming) Private Collection / © Look and Learn / Bridgeman Images.
p37 (hillfort) Werner Forman Archive / Bridgeman Images.